Eliminate Panic Attacks Forever
The Quick & Easy Solution

Having suffered with them myself for over 20 years, I understand how horrible they can be.

But you don't have to suffer with the debilitating effects of anxiety and panic attacks! There are things you can do to stop panic attacks and keep them from coming back forever!

— Elaine Andreessen

Eliminate Panic Attacks Forever
The Quick & Easy Solution

By Elaine Andreessen

Copyright © 2011 Elaine Andreessen

All rights reserved under International and Pan-American Copyright Conventions.

ISBN-13: 978-1456553661

ISBN-10: 1456553666

Table of Contents

Introduction 1

My Story 4

Chapter One: Causes of Anxiety 7

Chapter Two: Who Has Anxiety? 10

Chapter Three: Forms of Anxiety 13

    Generalized Anxiety Disorder (GAD) 13

    Social Anxiety Disorder 16

    Obsessive Compulsive Disorder 19

    Post-Traumatic Stress Disorder 22

Chapter Four: Panic Disorder 26

Chapter Five: Getting Help 32

Chapter Six: Medication 35

Chapter Seven: Therapy 44

Chapter Eight: Alternative Treatments 48

Chapter Nine: Make Treatments More Effective 51

Chapter Ten: Untreated Anxiety 53

Chapter Eleven: Preventing Panic 54

    Cut out Certain Foods 55

Chapter Twelve: Anxiety Support 59

Chapter Thirteen: A Panic Plan 63
    Step One: Change Your Diet 63
    Step Two: Halt Panic Quickly 63
    Step Three: Seek Medical Attention 64
    Step Four: Take Medication Briefly 65
    Step Five: Tell Yourself You Aren't Dying 66
Conclusion 69

"Panic and anxiety are figments of an overactive and nervous mind and nothing more…"

Introduction

Your heart is pounding fast and you are feeling dizzy. It seems as though you have to sit down in order for you not to fall. You are having trouble catching your breath. You are experiencing a numbing feeling in your hands and feet. There is a tightening pressure in your chest area. You think you may be on the verge of a heart attack. You think something is wrong with you; however, **you are far from dying**.

Anxiety is a mental disorder in which a person fears just about anything and they think every outcome will turn out for the worst. This fear is frightening because it is so intense and they always fear that someone is after them.

If you have any type of disorder that is associated with anxiety, then your mind will always be focused on being scared for no reason. You will always feel that there is no solution to your unfounded fear and that there is no way out.

You feel paralyzed as though you cannot do anything. Basically, you are frozen with fear. This disorder can attack at any time.

Anxiety disorder is more than just one action. Anxiety disorder has different sub-disorders that can fit under this. For instance, there are panic attacks, obsessive-compulsive disorder and others that are related to the anxiety disorder family.

Many people all over suffer from anxiety attacks. If you are not afflicted with them, you may know someone who is. If it is you, you need to know how to help yourself. If it's someone else, you need to know how to help them. You will have to be understanding and help them to get the treatment and support that they need to combat this condition.

My Story

I was just a kid when I first had a panic attack. I had no idea what was happening to me, but I knew I felt terrible.

At the time, it wasn't so bad. Because I was young, I had no real fear that I was having a heart attack. If I had, I'm sure the attack would have been much worse.

The first panic attack I remember was when I was about ten years old. I was out with friends and I suddenly felt very weak and dizzy. I began to sweat even though I wasn't particularly warm, and I had to sit down.

I couldn't understand why I was feeling so strangely. None of my friends were feeling this way. I had never felt this way before. All I knew was I felt awful.

These attacks continued off and on throughout my teenage years. I would have them once every few months, and always when I was in a large group of people.

As I entered adulthood, I began to have them more often. I started to get them at work, and when I was standing in line at the grocery store.

One day an attack was so bad I went to the emergency room feeling as though I was having a heart attack! Of course, they found nothing wrong.

After dozens of trips to the hospital, I was finally diagnosed with panic attacks. I was given Xanax, and it worked. Finally, I understood what was wrong with me, and I had something that could get rid of the attacks right away!

Of course, Xanax is highly addictive. I could not stay

on the medication forever. I began to see a therapist in order to try to wean me off medication.

Therapy did not work…

After years of suffering and tons of research, I finally came up with a method that worked to get rid of my panic attacks. I discovered a solution that worked where thousands of dollars of therapy could not!

In this book, you will learn what I did. I will teach you exactly how I got rid of my panic attacks, so you can do the same!

Chapter One: Causes of Anxiety

There is no one thing that causes this disorder and those that are related to it. You may think that there are certain things that trigger it. Well, there could be and then again, it may be something that just happens. It all depends on how it is perceived.

Those that the anxiety attacks or related disorders may have one attack. Then they may go back to the scene where the initial one took place and have another one. They are reminded of what happened before. They will feel bad and end up having another one without thinking about it. It seems like a constant cycle of intense fear. Then they feel that they will have more attacks.

Believe it or not, it's all in the mind. If you constantly fear and expect to have an anxiety attack or something related to it, then it will happen. The thing about this is people that experience these attacks resent having to hear that it's all in the mind. They feel that people are brushing this off as something that you can get over.

The feeling of anxiety comes from your brain. According to studies that deal with this, there are at least two areas of your brain that help to trigger the sense of fear and anxiety in your mind. It causes your brain to have a defense mechanism and then you react.

However, there can be situations that you may think cause anxiety and related attacks. Some people have so much stress nowadays. It can come from office politics, overwhelming debt, family issues and other events that can bring this on.

There are also some drugs that can trigger an anxiety attack from side effects or withdrawals. This would include alcohol, caffeine, cold medicine, decongestants, nicotine, diet pills and numerous other medications that people take for various ailments and illnesses.

Not eating right can also be a contributor to anxiety. There are some situations, where you may have to take a test or face a lot of people. If you're not ready, you can get nervous or jittery.

Chapter Two: Who Has Anxiety?

There is no certain group on this earth that is a target for anxiety and related attacks or disorders. So, with that said, who do you think suffers from this? Well, it could be anyone. It could be in your family, your friends, co-workers or anyone that you may know.

A lot of times, it could be those that you know and you would have never thought in a million years that they would suffer from something like this.

Unfortunately, these attacks are usually kept secret and not disclosed. This is one of those "sweep under the rug" embarrassment moments. This is not something that is talked about out in the open. Some people will acknowledge dealing with this when they are caught in the act and can't fake it.

Believe it or not, there are people such as politicians and even Hollywood celebrities who suffer from anxiety attacks and related conditions. However, they pay their publicists and others to keep it out of the public eye.
They don't want to be in the spotlight because they have to work on keeping up their image. However, what they may not realize is that someone may be able to benefit from their disclosure.

Unfortunately, for people that have to deal with this, anxiety attacks affect and tend to interfere with those who are trying to live a normal life. If you have excessive anxiety attacks, it can be related to a psychiatric condition. When these attacks become serious and they last a long time, they are considered to be out of the norm.

With the symptoms of an anxiety attack, the brain relays messages to other parts of a person's body. Certain parts of the body, such as the lungs and heart work overtime while the anxiety attack is happening. The brain ends up releasing a lot of adrenaline.

Adrenaline causes the "fight or flight" response. This is the body's natural response to stress. In the wild, an animal that experiences stress needs to prepare to defend itself or run away. The heart rate increases in order to make the senses work more efficiently. The animal may defecate or urinate in order to become lighter on its feet. These things cause the symptoms you feel during a panic attack.

Chapter Three: Forms of Anxiety

There are several different types of anxiety disorders. Let's take a look at some of the types.

Generalized Anxiety Disorder (GAD)

Generalized anxiety disorder, or GAD, deals with people that are constant worriers and are always tense. The thing about this is that there really isn't a cause for this, nor is anyone or anything at fault to provoke it. They look for the worst and are always extremely worried about work, family health and money. They even feel anxiety in the course of their normal day. If this pattern is consistent for at least six months, a person can be considered as suffering from GAD. They feel that they cannot stop worrying even though the concern is not as great as they make it out to be.

It's difficult for them to relax, they are easily startled by people or noises and they have a hard time focusing. Sometimes they cannot sleep at night or wake up in the morning on their own. Here are some other symptoms that contribute to generalized anxiety disorder:

- Feeling tired
- Aching muscles
- Irritability
- Diarrhea
- Nausea
- Vomiting
- Sweating
- Lightheadedness
- Shortness of breath
- Frequent trips to the bathroom

- Shaking or trembling
- Hot flashes

The symptoms can vary between individuals. Some people have all or most of these symptoms, and others have only a few.

If they don't have a high anxiety level and still suffer from generalized anxiety disorder, they can still be employed and be able to interact socially with others. However, if they have GAD on a higher scale, they may have trouble doing and completing simple tasks that others would take for granted.

Close to seven million American adults suffer from generalized anxiety disorders. There are more women (about twice as many) than men that are dealing with this. Even with that, the risk reaches its peak starting at childhood and going through the middle age years. Studies have shown that there are some genes that contribute to people getting GAD.

There are other anxiety disorders that happen in conjunction with GAD, such as substance abuse and depression. If treated properly, the person affected can overcome their worries with whatever problems they are dealing with.

Social Anxiety Disorder

Social anxiety disorder, which is also known as social phobia, happens when a person is extremely self-conscious and anxious. It happens every day in different social situations. They are extremely fearful of being watched.

They are also fearful of being judged by others. They try to be extremely careful and go out of their way to not do things that could cause them embarrassment.

For a while, they are extremely fearful prior to a situation that they feel can become a disaster. It can became so bad that they lose focus and can't think straight. With social anxiety disorder, they can allow this fear to cause them to lose focus.

It doesn't matter whether it happens at school, work or at home. Having social anxiety disorder can make it difficult for the person affected to cultivate relationships with others.

With social anxiety disorder, it may be somewhat difficult for people to get over their excessive fears and concerns. This is true even if they know that what they feel is not realistic. Some will try to make amends.

Even then there is a feeling of anxiety and they don't feel comfortable when they are around other people.

Then they are overly concerned of how others thought of them after the encounter.

A person could be in a social setting (for example, at dinner with someone or more than one person) and they will experience anxiety because they are fearful. They will sweat a lot, blush, shake, or find it difficult to hold a conversation with other people at the table. They always seem to feel that other people are watching them.

There are over 15 million adults in the United States alone that suffer from social anxiety disorder or social phobia. For the most part, this condition begins as a child and can continue through adolescence.

There are some studies that say genetics plays a part in this. This condition is often coupled with depression or other anxiety disorders or attacks. It is not a good idea for those affected to treat themselves with medication. It could make the situation worse. This is better treated with professionals that are experienced in this field.

Obsessive Compulsive Disorder

People that deal with obsessive-compulsive disorder, or OCD, constantly have thoughts that can make them upset. In order to get their anxiety under control, they use compulsions (rituals). However, the tables end up turning on them because the rituals take control over their mind.

For instance, there are some people that are obsessed with being clean. They are known as "clean freaks". Of course, it's a good practice to want everything to stay clean, but they can get to the point of being overly controlling about germs or dirty surfaces.

They have a compulsion to wash their hands continuously. They don't want any germs or dirt to touch their hands. When they go to the bathroom, they will take a paper towel to open and close the door, just to keep from getting germs on their hands.

If people that have OCD don't feel like they look their best, they will look in the mirror several times until they feel they are presentable. They don't want to feel as though they look out of place among others. These actions provide them with a temporary release of the anxiety that they have been feeling. People with this disorder are always compelled to check things repeatedly, or make sure that things are in the same place repeatedly.

Sometimes, they are obsessed with ideas of violence or harm to others. They also have thoughts of crazy things that people would not normally think about. There are times when they feel they have to hoard and keep things that they don't need.

There are some that have rituals in their home. One of the more common ones is checking the stove several times before they leave to make sure it is off. Having obsessive-compulsive disorder can turn into havoc and an unwelcome interruption when it happens on a daily basis.

When a person is engrained with obsessive-compulsive disorder, they know what they are doing doesn't make much sense, but they don't look at their behavior as something that is abnormal.

There are over two million adults in the United States that have obsessive-compulsive disorder. This condition does not stand out on its own. It can be combined with things such as anxiety disorders or attacks, depression or eating disorders.

This disorder affects women and men almost equally. It usually starts as a child or it can start in the teen years or even as an adults. Through research, there is an indication that OCD can happen through genetics. At least of third of all adults in the United States start out with OCD as a child.

The symptoms of obsessive-compulsive disorder can come and go at any time. If it really gets bad, it can severely affect a person from acting in a normal capacity and doing certain tasks. It's a good idea for those that are dealing with this not to use alcohol or drugs to calm them down. It just makes the situation worse for them.

There are certain treatments and medications that can be used to ward off obsessive-compulsive disorder. They can help people that are in fear or anxiety to be desensitized to what is going on around them.

Post-Traumatic Stress Disorder

Post-Traumatic Stress Disorder or PTSD happens when someone has suffered something that included harm of the body or implied the threat of harm. The person who gets PTSD may have been harmed, or it may have been someone close to them.

PTSD is commonly known in regard to veterans who served in a war. However, there are other things, such as a rape, kidnapping, abuse, vehicular accidents, plane crashes or natural disasters such as hurricanes or floods.

Those that suffer from Post-Traumatic Stress Disorder can be easily startled. They also have no feeling for those who they used to have a close relationship with. They start to have less interest in things they used to do. They show less affection, are increasingly aggressive and show more of the irritable side.

They try to block out things that remind them of that traumatic event instead of working through it. If the event was something that someone else deliberately acted on against them, then PTSD will greatly affect them.

Nightmares can haunt them and they start to see flashbacks such as sounds, feelings and images of what happened. There are sounds that can remind them of that event. For instance, if a door slams, then that could mean that someone has you trapped in a room and ready to pounce on you with their abuse. It could by physical or verbal. Some people don't realize that verbal abuse is just as bad, if not worse than physical abuse.

Keep in mind that everyone who has been traumatized will not experience PTSD. Some people are able to cope with what happened and move on. There are others that need therapy and medication to deal with their issues.

PTSD can start a few months after the event or incident. It could last for a few more months, or continue through the years. In order to be officially classified as PTSD, the symptoms have to continue for at least a month. There are some who end up having PTSD as a chronic condition.

There are over seven million adults in the United States that are dealing with Post-Traumatic Stress Disorder. It can start from the childhood years and work its way up to adulthood. There are more women that suffer from this than men. PTSD is also combined with substance abuse, depression or other anxiety disorders or attacks.

Chapter Four: Panic Disorder

Panic disorder is considered to be an illness. Symptoms include feeling suddenly terrorized, feeling faint, pain in the chest or feeling smothered. Panic attacks fall under the panic disorder condition and are prone to some of these same symptoms, plus others. When someone is having a panic attack, there are thoughts that are unrealistic or they fear that they are no longer in control or a situation.

With panic disorder, a person can also experience depression, or substance abuse. If these conditions are attached to their panic disorder, they should not be treated together. Sometimes they will feel sad or won't want to eat. They may not be able to sleep or only sleep for a few hours. They don't have much energy to do anything and they cannot maintain focus.

Panic Attacks

A panic attack is when a person has a fear or apprehension that is sudden or intense. There is usually nothing wrong and no one is in danger. Panic attacks can happen suddenly, last for a few minutes, and then it's over. There are others that last longer than a few minutes or there may be more than one and they follow behind one another.

There are three types of panic attacks:

Spontaneous –these panic attacks occur with no warning. There is nothing that could possibly bring it on. Even if a person is sleeping, they can still experience a panic attack.

Situationally bound – these panic attacks happen when there is a situation to which a person has been or will be exposed to. They are consider to trigger or provoke the panic attack. For instance, if a person hears a car backfire, it could remind them of when they were in the military and fighting a war with ammunition.

Situationally predisposed – these panic attacks can happen when there is a delayed reaction. The attack doesn't always occur right away. There are some instances where people may immediately have an attack, and other instances it is delayed or it may not happen at all.

Panic attacks are defined as having at least four or more symptoms:

- A choking feeling

- Lightheaded or dizzy

- Shaking

- Trembling

- Shortness of breath

- Accelerated heartbeat

- Pain in chest

- Numbness

- Chills

- Feeling of going crazy

- Nauseated

- Sweating

- Feelings of detachment

If a person experiences less than four symptoms, they can still be classified as having a panic attack, but it would be called a "limited symptom" panic attack. A person can have a panic attack at any time. It can even happen when they are sleeping. It has affected millions of adults in the United States.

However, there are more women that experience panic attacks. In fact, women experience panic attacks twice as much as men do. Panic attacks can start in the late teen or early adult years.

There are people that have frequent panic attacks and allow themselves to become almost helpless. There are some places where they will have stay away from because it can trigger another attack.

Or a person may not be able to participate in some activities, like going shopping and related outings. Most of the time, they are confined to where they live and won't go out unless someone else is with them.

This condition is called agoraphobia, which is when a person is fearful of open spaces or being out and about by themselves. If they seek help early for this, the progressive treatment can be successful.

It is a very treatable anxiety disorder and will respond to most medications or therapies that are provided to them. Medication and/or therapy can help the affected person to alter the way that they think in order to rid themselves of fear and anxiety.

If you have frequent panic attacks, you may have a panic disorder. Panic attacks become a panic disorder when the condition becomes chronic. Your life can be in serious danger, along with others.

Chapter Five: Getting Help

If you think you may be experiencing symptoms of an anxiety disorder, attack or related condition, please consult with your physician. He or she will be able to advise you if your symptoms match the clinical diagnosis of any of these mental health conditions.

If it is the case, you will need to consult with a professional that specializes in mental health conditions. These professionals are trained in therapy that deals with various behavioral patterns and will suggest medication if it is warranted.

Find one that you will be comfortable about discussing your condition with. You don't want to feel intimidated by their presence. You want to be relaxed and to be able to discuss what is going on with you. The mental health professional will work with you to devise a plan that will help you get over your struggles with these kinds of disorders and attacks.

If you are prescribed medication, you must take it as directed and don't stop unless you are advised by your physician. You and the mental health professional or your physician should discuss how the medication will work. If you have side effects, please consult them as soon as possible. They may have alter your dosage.

Concerning costs for medication and treatment, most insurance plans will cover that. However, do not assume and check with your insurance company first. If you lack insurance, check with your local or country government agency to seek mental health care at one of their facilities.

The governmental agencies usually stick to a sliding scale depending how much that you can pay. Alternatively, if you have public assistance, Medicaid may kick in to pay for these services.

Some areas have free mental health clinics that can help you. Check around to find out if your area has a clinic that can work on a sliding scale, or even offer free treatment. You may have to bring proof of need such as bank statements and paycheck stubs, so be prepared for that.

Chapter Six: Medication

For the most part, medication is used for anxiety attacks, disorders and related conditions. The choices can depend on what the condition is and what the person wants. A physician must conduct a thorough evaluation to determine if they are indeed suffering from one of these mental health conditions.

If so, it must also be established as to what type of disorder they are dealing with. If there is a combination of things, they must also be identified so that the physician will know how to treat it.

If they have already received treatment from an existing or a past anxiety disorder condition, the physician needs to know that. They also need to know if medication was given and the dosage.

Or if they had other treatment, that needs to be disclosed as well. If there were any side effects, that should be included, along with any therapy that was provided and if it was beneficial for them.

There are some people that feel that the treatment they received did not work for them. Sometimes, it could be they may not have had enough time for the process to change or it was not done correctly. Some people may have to go through different medications or treatments to find what will work for them.

Medication is not the cure all for anxiety disorders, attacks and related conditions. However, medication can control these conditions while the person is receiving therapy. Medication can only be used if a physician prescribes it.

They are usually prescribed by psychiatrists that offer therapy of work with colleagues that provide some of the same services. For the most part, the medications that are used for anxiety disorders are:

- Antidepressants

- Anti-anxiety drugs

- Beta-blockers

Using any of these medications can help the person to live a normal life.

Antidepressants

Originally, antidepressants were used for treatment of depression. However, they also work for those that are suffering from anxiety disorders. They work to change the chemistry in the brain. Once the initial dose is taken, it takes at least 4 to 6 weeks before the symptoms will go away. The medication must be taken as directed in order for this to work.

SSRIs – Selective Serotonin Reuptake Inhibitors – these antidepressants work to change the level of the communication of the brain cells. Some of the more common ones are Prozac, Zoloft and Lexapro.

They are used to treat any panic disorder that is mixed with social phobia, depression or OCD. Since these are newer, they don't have as many side effects. However, those that use them may experience being jittery or nauseated in the initial stages of taking them. This is only temporary.

Tricyclics – These antidepressants are older than SSRIs and are used for anxiety disorders other than OCD. They are administered with a low dosage and increase gradually.

Side effects include being dizzy, dry mouth, drowsy and weight gain. This can be eliminated by adjusting the dosage or using another medication of the same kind of antidepressant. Tofranil is used for GAD and panic disorder; Anafranil is used for OCD.

MAOIs – Monoamine Oxidase Inhibitors – these are the oldest of the antidepressants available to use for these conditions. It is mostly used for anxiety disorders, attacks and related conditions.

Some of the more common ones are Nardil, Marplan and Parnate. When taking MAOIs, there are certain foods and drinks that you have to stay away from. That would include cheese and red wine.

In addition to that, you cannot take Advil, Motrin, Tylenol or any other pain, cold or allergy reliever medication. Plus, women will not be able to use certain types of birth control pills.

Herbal supplements are also off limits. Mixing MAOIs with any of these can cause an adverse reaction.

Anti-Anxiety Drugs – Drugs such as benzodiazepines are highly potent. They work to fight off anxiety and have very few side effects. Being drowsy is the only one that is noticeable. This drug is only prescribed for a brief period of time. Physicians are weary about providing them to past drug abusers.

Because people can get easily addicted to them, they look for additional doses so they can keep going. However, if the person has panic disorder, they can use these drugs up to a year.

For social phobia, Klonpin is used and Ativan is used for panic disorder. One of the most common antidepressants on the market is Xanax, which is used for GAD and panic disorder.

If a person stops taking benzodiazepines all of a sudden, they can experience withdrawals; the anxiety attacks can come back to haunt them. This is one reason why some physicians are leery about using this drug or use them sporadically.

Another anti-anxiety medication is Busiprone and it is used for GAD. There are some side effects that include nausea, headaches or dizziness. This is taken different than benzodiazepines. Busiprone has to be taken every day for at least two week before a person will feel the anti-anxiety effect from the drug.

Beta-Blockers – Beta-blockers are used for treatment of heart conditions. They can also be used to keep away physical symptoms that determine anxiety disorders. Beta-blockers are used in situations such as if a person is giving a speech in front of other people, a bet-blocker can be used to keep those symptoms at bay.

If you are taking medication for an anxiety disorder, you should do the following:

- Have your physician to advise you on what medication would be effective for your condition.
- Have the physician consult you on how the drug works and what are the side effects from taking the drug.
- Inform your physician of other medications you may be taking. They may interfere with the dosage of the drug anxiety disorders.
- The physician should advise you on the dosage and how you are directed to take it. They also need to advise you on how you should stop taking it when the time comes. With medication,

some of them can actually trigger systems that can cause panic attacks. Physicians should always start out with a lower dose and then work their way up.

Chapter Seven: Therapy

Psychotherapy deals with interacting with a mental health professional, such as a psychologist, psychiatrist or someone who is trained in counseling of mental health issues and conditions. They can help to find out what triggers anxiety disorders and panic disorders. They also work to see what is the best path to take in order to combat the symptoms.

Cognitive-Behavioral Therapy

Cognitive-Behavioral Therapy, or CBT, is very effective in the treatment of anxiety disorders. Thinking patterns are changed with the cognitive portion. The way people react to anxiety related issues is the behavioral portion.

People that have panic disorder can use cognitive-behavioral therapy to distinguish between heart attacks and panic attacks. CBT can also be used to help them overcome social phobia. It can help them to realize that everyone is not watching your every move, nor is everyone judging them.

There are techniques that they can learn to use for positive exposure. These techniques will also help them not to be so sensitive about anxiety triggers and symptoms.

Therapy for those who suffer from is to get them to have contact with germs or dirt on their hands. They should wait around a while before they wash them. The therapist will help them deal with the anxiety that follows before they wash their hands. The more they do it, the more the anxiety goes away.

If a person suffers from social phobia, their therapy would be to spend time with others in social situations. They should resist trying to leave when they start to feel uncomfortable. They won't feel ashamed or feel that people are judging them.

If someone has PTSD, their therapy could be drumming up that event that caused them a lot of trauma and pain in their life. This can help to diminish the fear that they are feeling inside.

With cognitive-behavioral therapy, the therapists will provide ways of how you can implement deep breathing exercises and other exercises to get rid of anxiety. Exercises can help you to relax in tense and stressful situations.

Phobias have been treated with behavioral therapy that forces a person to expose themselves in a way that brings out their true fears and apprehensions. The face up to whatever it was that they feared.

It may be looking at photos or listening to voices on tape. It could also mean a face-to-face encounter with that person. The therapist will accompany them for support so that they can face their fears head on.

With CBT, this therapy must connect directly with the anxieties of the person and geared toward what they need. The only thing that will affect them is how uncomfortable they will feel because of the heightened anxiety. However, that is only temporary.

This type of therapy lasts for about three months or 12 weeks. It can be done as a one-on-one, or it can be with a group of people that are suffering from similar conditions. For social phobia, group therapy is better because a person will have to interact with other people. For certain anxiety disorders, medication may be required in order for the treatment to be effective.

Chapter Eight: Alternative Treatments

Other than taking medication and therapy, there are alternative treatments that can be used in order to combat these conditions in the anxiety and panic attack family.

One of the main keys to getting over anxiety and panic attacks is to relax. That's not as easy to do as some may think. Start out by focusing and making sure that you are breathing slowly and steadily.

When a person is having a panic attack, one of the first things that happens is they have trouble breathing. Sometimes they have to pant in order to catch their breath. The purpose here is to make your breaths even so that they will slow down your heart rate.

This will help the panic attack to eventually go away. A person is able to calm themselves by breathing slowly. They must continue to release air from their lungs. This helps to have deep breaths and make them feel calmer.

Lying down with your backside near a wall, bend the knees with the feet against the wall. Use one foot at a time and press into the wall. As you press it in, breathe in. As you release it from the wall, breathe out. Change up your feet when you are doing this. Take about 15 minutes until the feeling of panic has lifted from you.

Try not to think about the past. A lot of times, panic attacks happen from something that has to do with your past that you were upset about. Look at different shapes and colors. If you like pets, get a small dog or cat and love on it.

If you are into fragrances, you can use aromatherapy to relieve yourself of anxiety and panic attacks. One aroma that has a calming effect is lavender. There are many places where you can purchase essential oils.

When you feel an anxiety or panic attack coming on, sniff the oil and it will work to calm you down. You can also use it as a massage oil, along with olive or grape seed oil. There are other aromatherapy oils you can use. You have to smell them to see which one you prefer.

Chapter Nine: Make Treatments More Effective

There are independent support groups that you can join. You will be able to share your knowledge and experience with those who are dealing with similar problems. There are also chat rooms online.

However, this has to be done with caution. Not everything someone says about anxiety and panic attacks are the gospel. You can also seek the counsel of your pastor of minister of the cloth. However, you need to make sure that you seek counseling from a trained mental health professional.

There are also meditation and techniques that deal with managing stress. This can help those with these disorders so that you can stay calm and focused. This can also help with your therapy. As you are finding ways to find peace within yourself, there are some things that you should avoid consuming.

They would include beverages that have caffeine, illegal drugs and some cold and sinus medications from over the counter. They can actually provoke the symptoms of anxiety and panic disorders.

Your family is crucial to have in your life in order for you to make a full recovery. They should be supportive and help you in every way they can. However, there may be some family members that may want to deride and ridicule you.

They may tend to think that is trivial and has no merit. You may have speak with them and get them to understand that this is a serious condition. If they still refuse, then move on and find some friends that will have your back and provide you with the support that you need.

Chapter Ten: Untreated Anxiety

Panic attacks can continue for a long time, sometimes for years to come. This longevity can be complicated by having consistent attacks. Symptoms include having certain phobias (fears) or leaving outside the home, not wanting to be around other people, feeling suicidal, financial issues and substance abuse. As a results, the person could end up suffering from heart disease.

If the panic attacks are not treated, the anxiety can increase and get worse. Their daily routine may be affected by attacks that are not going away. This must be dealt with head on; otherwise, the person cannot be a productive citizen of society.

Chapter Eleven: Preventing Panic

There are ways that you can decrease the chance of an onset of a panic attack. You can learn how to deal with them better. You must recognize the symptoms. When the initial ones begin, they may be others that come along. Just remember to take slow and deep breaths.

Keep decreasing you anxiety level through things such as exercise and meditation. Don't be in a rush and take your time with this. Doing it quickly can defeat the purpose. Therapy is a time consuming process and improvement will be gradual.

Don't be hard on yourself. Take it easy. Don't beat yourself
over the head criticizing yourself because of your condition. Make sure that you avoid things such as cigarettes, teas that have caffeine, and carbonated

drinks. That may be difficult, but at least start weaning your way off slowly.

Work on not thinking about things that may have been traumatic for you in the past. These traumatic events can shape how you will react to things in the future. You cannot allow the past to hinder you if you are looking to move forward.

Make sure to keep a loving and understanding support system around you so that you will be able to move forward every day. Whether it's family members or a friend, they need to be genuinely interested in help you get better and relieve those fears that you have pent up inside.

Cut out Certain Foods

There are certain foods that make panic attacks worse. It's important to change your diet in order to avoid these foods, however, do not cut them all out at once. You need to figure out what makes your panic attacks worse, so you can avoid only those that actually affect you.

Caffeine – It is extremely important to avoid caffeine if you have any type of anxiety disorder. Caffeine is one of the most prevalent causes of anxiety, and in people who are prone to anxiety attacks, it will almost always cause or exacerbate panic attacks.

Remember to avoid hidden sources of caffeine. Caffeine can be found in coffee, tea, many types of cola drinks (including many you wouldn't think of, so ALWAYS read the label), chocolate, and weight control medications.

Caffeine causes lactic acid to build up in the blood, which can increase anxiety.

Sugar – In some people, sugar can cause anxiety. Like caffeine, sugar can cause lactic acid to build up in the blood, increasing anxiety. Try to limit sugar intake.

Additionally, the symptoms of candidiasis (systemic yeast infection) mimic the symptoms of panic attacks. Some people who are suffering from anxiety are actually suffering from candidiasis.

If you think you may have a candida overgrowth, try this. Immediately after you wake up, before you drink or brush your teeth, spit into a glass of water. If the spit dissolves immediately or floats on top of the water, you probably do not have a yeast problem. If it floats on top but sends out little tendrils into the water that look like jellyfish tentacles, you DO have a yeast problem. This could be causing a lot of your anxiety.

If you have yeast overgrowth, you may need to use a special diet and potentially see your doctor for medication like Nystatin to control the yeast.

Alcohol – Alcohol is used by many people to calm down, but in some people it can cause anxiety. It causes lactic acid to build up in the blood just like sugar and caffeine.

Wheat Gluten – Many people are sensitive to wheat gluten and don't even realize it. Severe wheat gluten sensitivity is called celiac disease. The symptoms of celiac disease are similar to those of panic attacks. Try cutting wheat out of your diet for a while to see if symptoms improve.

Chapter Twelve: Anxiety Support

If you are helping someone who has one of these conditions, it is very important that you are there for the long haul. It may take longer than a few weeks or months for that person to totally overcome this.

You should not be judgmental or condescending in any way to the person who is suffering. This is a serious matter and you should treat it as such. The worst thing you could do regarding anxiety and panic attacks is to be dismissive and think that they can quickly get over it. You cannot be the savior for them and solve their problem.

People who suffer these kinds of attacks are not thinking about anything except how scared they are that something bad is going to happen. The situation cannot be solved by shaking them and making them come out of it, or waving a magic wand over them and saying "abracadabra".

Don't underestimate their actions by thinking that they are pretending to be acting. This is serious and their actions should not be underestimated. The best thing you can do is to do everything in your power that you can to be there as that support system.

They could feel at any moment that they were in grave danger. They feel as though they could not pull themselves out of whatever trouble they perceived. This is when the accelerated heartbeat, shortness of breath and other symptoms come in to play.

If you ignore them, you are doing more to hurt them than to help. They depend on your support and if you decide to bail out on their weakest moment, they will feel more worthless.

This could make them start feeling depressed and not want to do much of anything for their situation. If they know that you are with them to help them stick it out, then they will feel better about themselves.

You must allow them to go through the attack. If you try to intervene, you could make the situation worse. Let it happen and they will eventually come out of it. However, if for some reason they don't stop, call a paramedic to assist.

One thing that you don't want to do is to give them medication, especially if it's not prescribed by their physician. That will definitely cause them harm. So make sure that you are not doing anything to jeopardize their well-being.

Where is hope for those who have been suffering for a long time with anxiety disorders, attacks, and panic attacks. You have to be willing to make the move to make changes in your life. There are other people out there that are suffering just like you.

However, your situation doesn't have to stay this way forever. There is help out there in the form of medication, and therapy. You just have to want it for yourself. The sooner you get the help, the better you will get. Once you do that, you will stop allowing these conditions to control your life.

Chapter Thirteen: A Panic Plan

Now that you understand more about your panic attacks, I'm going to give you a quick plan you can use to eliminate your panic attacks in 3 days or less. This will work for almost everyone!

Step One: Change Your Diet

You must change your diet immediately. Cut out caffeine immediately, as it is one of the most common dietary causes of anxiety. Then start cutting out other items that can cause anxiety.

Step Two: Halt Panic Quickly

One way to nip a panic attack in the bud right away is to splash your face with cold water. I know it sounds unusual, but the body has a mechanism that causes the heart rate and respiration to slow down if it thinks you are drowning. This is meant to help keep you alive longer if you're drowning, but you can use this to stop a panic attack.

Take some very cold tap water in your hands. Take a deep breath in an out slowly, then lower your face into your hands. Leave your face in the cold water as long as you can. This can help trick your body into thinking you are drowning, which can slow down a racing heart and end a panic attack.

Step Three: Seek Medical Attention

I know it's embarrassing to think about visiting the emergency room only to be told you're just having a panic attack. Believe me, I've been there! However, it will accomplish two very important things.

1. It will help ensure you're not really having a medical emergency.

2. It will help convince you that it really is just a panic attack.

When you have a lot of anxiety that causes physical symptoms, sometimes the fear that your symptoms might be a heart attack or another potentially deadly condition can exacerbate the anxiety. This can lead to a panic attack that spirals out of control.
If you receive medical help, the tests may prove nothing is physically wrong with you. This can help convince you that you are not going to die, which will help you bring the panic attack to a halt.

Step Four: Take Medication Briefly

Many anxiety medications are highly addictive, but they can be extremely effective at stopping a panic attack quickly. Alprazolam, known by its brand name Xanax, is one of the most addictive, but it is also very effective. Clonazepam, known by the name Klonopin, is much less addictive, but does not work as well for some people.

Medications like this should generally only be used briefly because of their potential for addiction, however they are very useful for showing you that you don't have a life-threatening condition. You can use medications to prove to your mind that your condition is not deadly, which can prevent future attacks. A heart attack would not be stopped by an anxiety medication, and when your symptoms stop after taking it, you will be more assured that you aren't dying.

Step Five: Tell Yourself You Aren't Dying

Whenever you feel the symptoms of anxiety coming, you must learn to immediately recognize it as anxiety and not something deadly. As soon as you begin to feel the symptoms, tell yourself, "It's only anxiety. It's nothing serious."

Here are some tips for telling the difference between anxiety and heart problems:

- Look at your fingernail beds. If your fingernails are extremely blue, something is physically wrong.

- Take an anti-anxiety drug. If it helps, it's just anxiety.

- Does your chest feel like an elephant is sitting on it? If you have a racing or palpitating heart, it's not necessarily a problem. If you feel like something very large is crushing your chest, get to an emergency room just in case.

- Are you having chest pain that lasts longer than 10 minutes? A heart attack will generally last a long time, but panic attack pain is usually brief. However, the racing heart can last longer.

- Are you experiencing tingling? If so, where is it? In a heart attack, tingling is generally felt only in the left arm. If you are feeling tingling elsewhere, it is probably just anxiety.

- Are you vomiting? Vomiting is possible during panic attacks, but it is more common during heart attacks.

If in doubt, visit a hospital. Even if nothing is physically wrong, simply being told so will often be enough to stop a panic attack.

Conclusion

Follow the panic plan first. This will help you get rid of your attacks quickly. After the attacks are gone, you can use the information in the rest of the book to ensure they don't return.

Remember these tips:

- Remember to cut out caffeine and other problem foods immediately, as these foods are extremely common triggers for panic attacks.

- Cut as much stress out of your life as possible. See a therapist if you have a lot of stress you cannot eliminate.

- Don't be afraid to seek medical treatment. Learning you aren't dying is a great step to stopping panic attacks.

I wish you the best of luck in getting rid of your panic attacks. I got rid of mine, and I know you can do the same.